Logic Brain Boosters

by
Becky Daniel

illustrated by Nancee McClure

Cover by Nancee McClure

Copyright © Good Apple, 1992

GOOD APPLE
1204 BUCHANAN ST., BOX 299
CARTHAGE, IL 62321-0299

S I M O N & S C H U S T E R *A Paramount Communications Company*

Copyright © Good Apple, 1992

ISBN No. 0-86653-652-3

Printing No. 9876

Good Apple, Inc.
299 Jefferson Road
P.O. Box 480
Parsippany, NJ 07054-0480

Table of Contents

GA1347

Introduction

Logic Brain Boosters is a collection of logic-based puzzles, activities and work sheets especially designed to make children think! *Webster's Dictionary* defines logic as "correct reasoning; sound thinking; the science that deals with the rules of correct reasoning and with proof by reasoning; a way of reasoning." Often many elementary lessons involve a great deal of rote learning, and one problem facing educators is how to teach our children to think analytically. Children can often read and write words that they do not comprehend, and although memorization is an important skill, thinking logically is important, too.

To prepare your students to use the work sheets found herein, it is important to remember that reading the directions may be difficult or impossible for beginning readers. It is therefore suggested that the directions be given in small groups and the example carefully explained before children are sent back to their desks to do independent seatwork.

Logic Brain Boosters will give children an opportunity to sharpen their deductive reasoning skills. When working these puzzles, children are required to recognize certain facts and deduce conclusions based on reasoning. The wide range of activities, from simple to complex, will give learners concrete practice in logical thinking that they may never otherwise receive. The activities in this book require children not only to deduce answers from given possibilities, but will also provide a framework for them to more easily move through the deductive process. Therefore, many answers will vary. The fun-filled puzzles, coloring activities, and activity sheets will make learning to think logically an enjoyable experience for all.

Bonus activities are found on most pages. These activities are usually more difficult and should not be a requirement. You may choose to use the bonus activities for extra credit. Students who complete these should receive special recognition. A class competition could involve keeping track of how many bonus activities are completed by each student and rewarding those who complete a given number. Awards are found on pages 59 and 60 and a special award certificate for bonus activities is included.

GA1347

Search and See

Find and color the matching designs the same color.

Bonus: Draw and color three pairs of matching designs.

GA1347

Exactly Alike

Complete each pair of things in the boxes found below so that they are exactly alike.

Bonus: Draw two things that are almost exactly alike. See if a friend can find the small differences between the two things.

GA1347

One! Two! Go!

Only two scarecrows on this page are exactly alike. Find and circle the two matching scarecrows.

Bonus: Draw two scarecrows that are exactly alike.

3

Mystery Maze

There are three paths through this maze. Find and color each path a different color.

Bonus: Draw a maze with three different paths.

4

GA1347

Sorting It Out!

Using each word clue, circle the appropriate pair of pictures in each row found below.

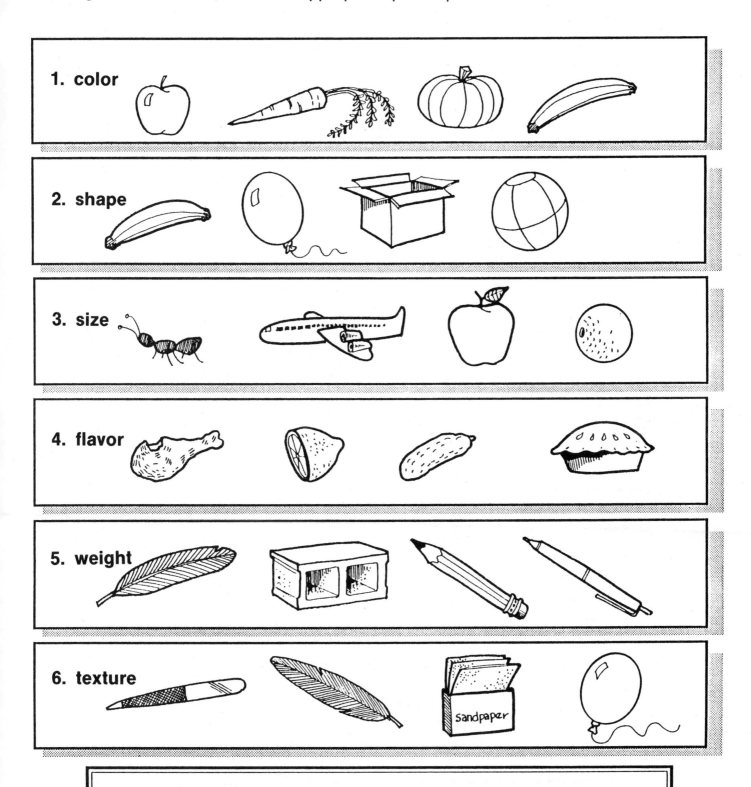

1. color

2. shape

3. size

4. flavor

5. weight

6. texture

sandpaper

Bonus: Write the explanation for each of your choices above.

GA1347

You Decide

Use the letters of the objects found below to answer each question.

1. **Which two objects are round?** _____

2. **Which two objects are animals?** _____

3. **Which three objects are things you can eat?** _____

4. **Which objects grow?** _____

5. **Which objects could be red?** _____

6. **Which objects weigh more than a marshmallow?** _____

Bonus: Describe one way C and E are alike. Different.

GA1347

Putting It in Order

Number the sentences found below in order from 1 to 6 to make a recipe for apple-sauce.

Remove seeds and core.

Wash apples.

Put into a pot with water and sugar and simmer for 30 minutes.

Cut apples into quarters.

Mash cooked apples with fork.

Let cool.

Bonus: Write steps 7 and 8 for this same recipe.

GA1347

Similarities

Use the words found in the Word Box below to tell how the objects in each box are similar to each other.

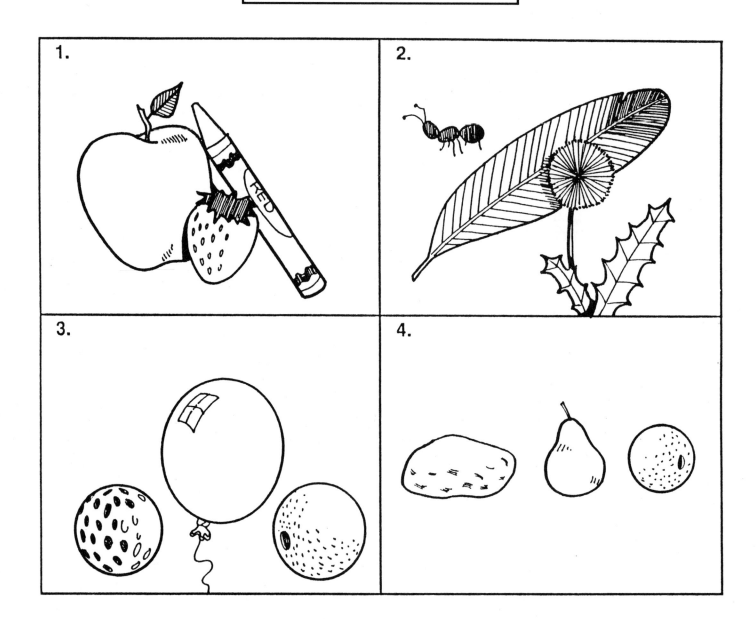

WORD BOX	
color	shape
size	weight

1.

2.

3.

4.

Bonus: Draw three objects that are similar in three of the four ways found in the Word Box.

GA1347

What's Next?

Use the row of designs found below to draw the appropriate shape to answer each question.

1. What comes after the ★ ? _____

2. What comes after the ● ? _____

3. What comes before the ✳ ? _____

4. What comes before the ● ? _____

5. What came before the shape that came before the ♥ ?

_____

6. What came before the shape that came before the ★ ?

_____

7. What came after the shape that came after the ★ ?

_____

8 What came after the shape that came after the ♥ ?

_____

Bonus: What shape came before the shape that came after the ★?

9

GA1347

Pick Carefully

Draw a picture or write the number for each appropriate object to answer the questions found below.

1. **Which objects are heavier than a tomato?** _____

2. **Which objects are larger than a marshmallow?** _____

3. **Which objects could be the same color as a strawberry?** _____

4. **Which objects are not shaped like an orange?** _____

5. **Which objects could be the same color as a yam?** _____

6. **Which objects are smaller than your hand?** _____

Bonus: Tell three ways popcorn and peanuts are alike and three ways they are different.

Calendar Work

Use the days on the calendar found below to answer each question.

SUN.	MON.	TUES.	WED.	THURS.	FRI.	SAT.
1	2	3	4	5	6	7

1. **If today is Sunday, tomorrow will be** _____ .

2. **If today is Wednesday, yesterday was** _____ .

3. **If today is Saturday, tomorrow will be** _____ .

4. **If today is Thursday, the day before yesterday was** _____ .

5. **If yesterday was Monday, tomorrow will be** _____ .

6. **If tomorrow will be Thursday, yesterday was** _____ .

Bonus: If the day after tomorrow will be Saturday, what was the day before yesterday?

GA1347

Putting It Together

Draw a picture of something you could make with the four things listed in each box.

dough
pepperoni slices
tomato sauce
cheese

1.

pumpkin
knife
candle
match

2.

dough
chocolate chips
baking sheet
oven

3.

popcorn
melted caramels
peanuts
small prize

4.

Bonus: Write the step-by-step directions for making any one of the four things you drew.

Always, Sometimes, Never

Use the number for each object to answer the questions found below.

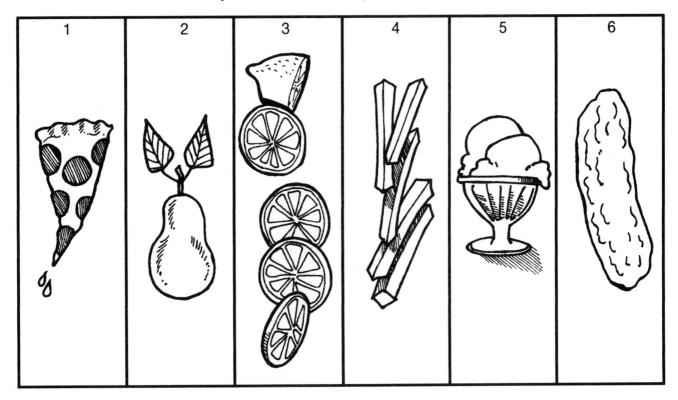

1. **Which object is something that is ALWAYS sour?**_____

2. **Which object is something that is sometimes SOUR?**_____

3. **Which object is something that is ALWAYS cold?**_____

4. **Which object is something SOMETIMES served with catsup?**_____

5. **What object is ALWAYS grown on a tree?** _____

6. **Which object is ALWAYS used to make lemonade?**_____

7. **Which object is ALWAYS made with cheese?** _____

8. **Which object is NEVER baked before serving?** _____

Why?_____

Bonus: Write an ALWAYS, a SOMETIMES, and a NEVER sentence.

GA1347

Or, And, Not

Use the words *or*, *and* or *not* to complete each sentence found below.

1. Balloons _____ apples are usually round.

2. Bananas, _____ carrots are a fruit.

3. Boys _____ girls like to play outdoors.

4. Marshmallows _____ whipped cream make a good topping for hot chocolate.

5. My mother _____ my father will drive the car to the park.

6. Hens, _____ roosters lay eggs.

7. My sister, _____ my brother wore my new dress without asking.

8. We will drink both orange juice _____ milk with our breakfast.

Bonus: Write an OR, an AND and a NOT sentence.

GA1347

Picture It!

Each square of the picture is represented by a letter and a number. For example: is B1. Write the appropriate letter and number on each picture square found below.

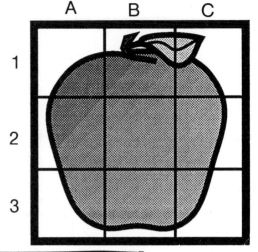

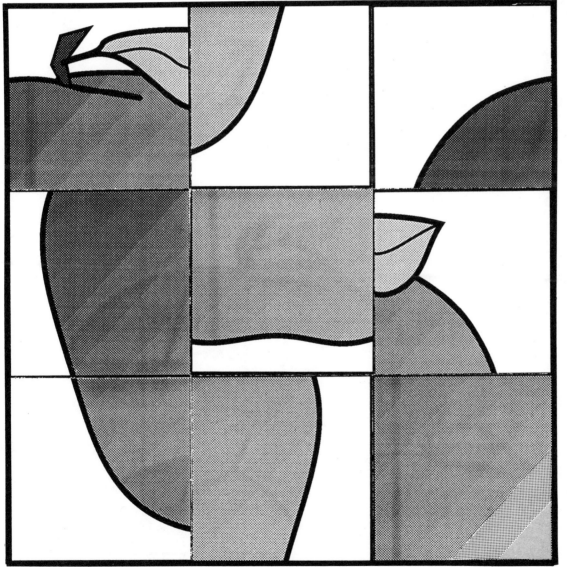

Bonus: Using a letter and a number, name this picture square.

GA1347

Color It First!

Begin this page by coloring each design the appropriate color. Then use the number for each colored shape to answer the questions found below.

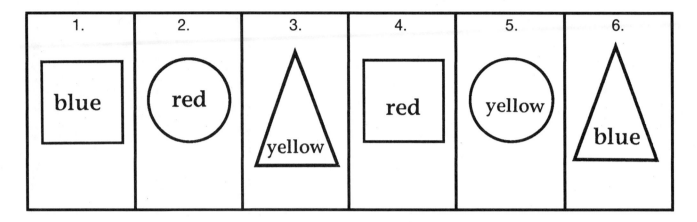

1. Which two shapes are round?_____

2. Which two shapes have four sides?_____

3. Which two shapes are yellow? _____

4. Which shape is the same color as number one? _____

5. Which shape is the same shape as number five?_____

6. Which two shapes have three sides? _____

7. Which two shapes placed one on top of the other would look like this?___

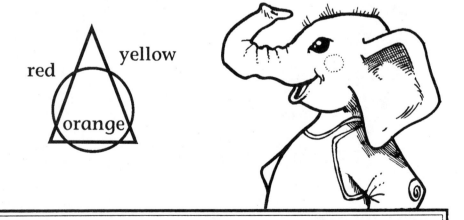

Bonus: Draw and color a picture of what number four and number five would look like if one were placed on top of the other.

16

GA1347

Add One

Begin this page by coloring each shape the appropriate color. Study each row of colored shapes to discover the pattern. Then draw and color a shape that logically follows in each row found below. The first one has been done for you.

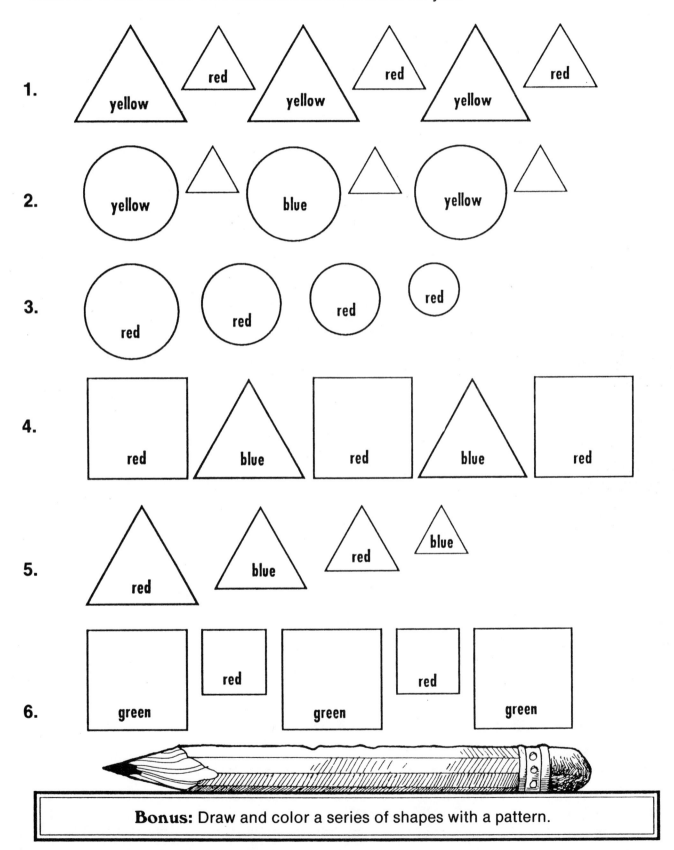

Bonus: Draw and color a series of shapes with a pattern.

GA1347

All, Most, Some, None

Eight children were asked how they felt about five different kinds of pie: apple, cherry, pumpkin, lemon and banana cream. Each favorable vote received a square on the graph. Use the graph found below to answer each question with the words *all*, *most*, *some* or *none*.

APPLE							
CHERRY							
PUMPKIN							
LEMON							
BANANA CREAM							

1. _____ of the children liked apple pie.

2. _____ of the children liked cherry pie.

3. _____ of the children liked lemon pie.

4. _____ of the children liked pumpkin pie.

5. _____ of the children liked banana cream pie.

6. _____ of the children didn't like pumpkin pie.

7. _____ of the children didn't like apple pie.

8. _____ of the children didn't like banana cream pie.

Bonus: Ask eight friends how they feel about these five pies and create your own pie graph.

GA1347

Chosen Colors

Eight children were asked how they felt about six different colors: red, blue, yellow, brown, pink and orange. Each favorable vote received a square on the graph. Example: all eight liked the color RED. Use the graph to complete each sentence with the words *all*, *most*, *some* or *none*.

RED								
BLUE								
YELLOW								
BROWN								
PINK								
ORANGE								

1. _____ of the children liked blue.

2. _____ of the children liked orange.

3. _____ of the children liked brown.

4. _____ of the children liked pink.

5. _____ of the children liked red.

6. _____ of the children like pink and yellow.

7. _____ of the children disliked red.

8. _____ of the children disliked brown.

Bonus: Which color did NONE of the children say they disliked?

19

GA1347

Size, Shape and Weight

Use the number of the pictures found to answer each question.

1. **Which object is about the same size and shape as a bubblegum ball?** _____

2. **Which object is about the same size and shape as an orange?** _____

3. **Which objects are small enough to carry in your pocket?** _____

4. **Which object would probably be the heaviest?** _____

5. **Which object would probably be the lightest?** _____

6. **Which object would probably be the largest?** _____

7. **Which object would probably be the smallest?** _____

8. **List the number of the objects in order from smallest to largest.** _____

_____

Bonus: List the number of the objects in order from lightest to heaviest.

Button, Button

Use the number of each group of buttons to answer the questions found below.

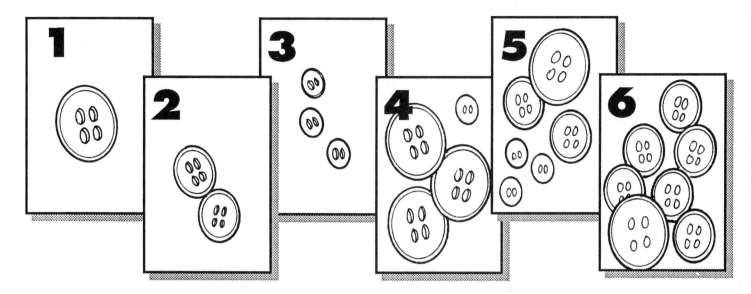

1. **In which group are MOST of the buttons middle-sized?**_____

2. **In which group are ALL of the buttons small?** _____

3. **In which group are MOST of the buttons big?** _____

4. **In which group are ALL of the buttons middle-sized?** _____

5. **In which group are NONE of the buttons small or middle-sized?** _____

6. **In which group are SOME of the buttons middle-sized?**_____

Bonus: Using all three words *most*, *all* and *some*, describe the buttons in one box.

GA1347

Six Kids

Study the picture of the children found below. Then use the words *all*, *some* or *none* to complete each sentence found below.

SUE   JULIE   TOM   MIKE   BOB   TEX

1. _____ of the children are taller than Tex.

2. _____ of the boys are shorter than Julie.

3. _____ of the children are shorter than Sue.

4. _____ of the children are taller than Sue.

5. _____ of the girls are taller than Tom.

6. _____ of the children are shorter than Tex.

Bonus: Write an *all*, a *some* and a *none* sentence about the children.

GA1347

Just Three, Please

To make the objects pictured in the boxes below, what would you need? In each box is a list of six things. Circle the three that you think are the most important for creating the object pictured.

1.

popcorn
pan
heat
milk
sugar
butter

2.

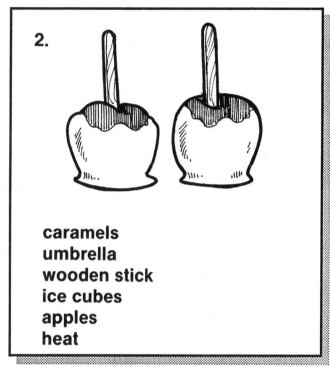

caramels
umbrella
wooden stick
ice cubes
apples
heat

3.

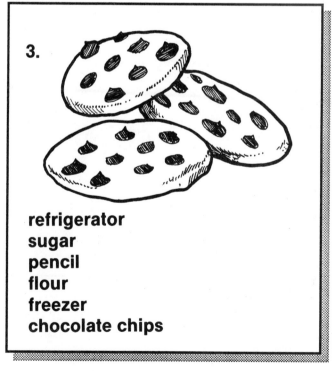

refrigerator
sugar
pencil
flour
freezer
chocolate chips

4.

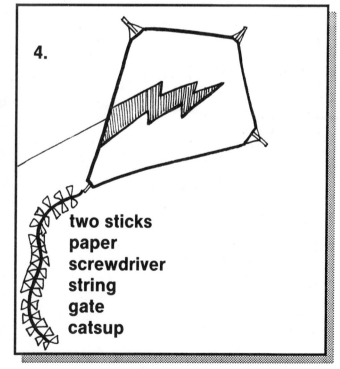

two sticks
paper
screwdriver
string
gate
catsup

Bonus: Draw a picture and then list the things you would need to make it.

GA1347

Make a List

Look at each treat pictured below. List everything you can think of that is needed to make it.

1.

1. _____
2. _____
3. _____
4. _____

2.

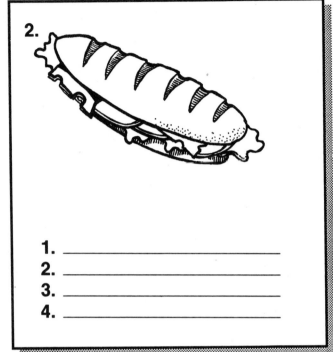

1. _____
2. _____
3. _____
4. _____

3.

1. _____
2. _____
3. _____
4. _____

4.

1. _____
2. _____
3. _____
4. _____

Bonus: Draw a picture of your favorite food and list all of the things needed to make it.

GA1347

Draw Them!

Read and follow the directions found in each box below.

1. Draw something stickier than a caramel apple.	**2. Draw something sweeter than bubble gum.**
3. Draw something hotter than hot chocolate.	**4. Draw something more sour than a lemon.**
5. Draw something spicier than a pizza.	**6. Draw something colder than ice cream.**

Bonus: Draw a dessert that is hot and cold at the same time.

Just Before

Use a sentence or phrase to answer each question found below.

1. **What do you do just before you put on your shoes?**

   _____

2. **What do you do just before you eat a candy bar?**

   _____

3. **What do you do just before you roller skate down the street?**

   _____

4. **What do you do just before you build a snowman?**

   _____

5. **What do you do just before you take a bath?**

   _____

6. **What do you do just before you brush your teeth?**

   _____

7. **What do you do just before you go to sleep at night?**

   _____

8. **What do you do just before you read a book?**

   _____

Bonus: Write one sentence that tells something you do just before something else.

GA1347

The First Thing

Use a sentence or phrase to answer each question found below.

1. **What is the first thing you do right after you open your eyes in the morning?**

   _____

2. **What is the first thing you do right after you put on your socks?**

   _____

3. **What is the first thing you do right after you wash your hands?**

   _____

4. **What is the first thing you do right after you say the Pledge of Allegiance?**

   _____

5. **What is the first thing you do right after you get home from school?**

   _____

6. **What is the first thing you do right after you turn on the television?**

   _____

7. **What is the first thing you do right after you sit down at your school desk?**

   _____

8. **What is the first thing you do right after you open a book?**

   _____

Bonus: Write a sentence about the first thing you do right after something.

27

GA1347

Est, Est, Est!

Use the number of the objects found below to answer each question.

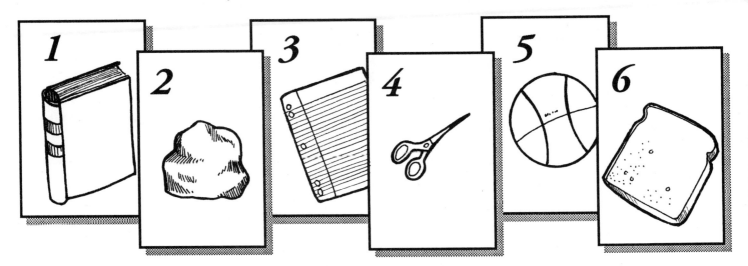

1. **Which object is the thickest?** _____

2. **Which object is the thinnest?** _____

3. **Which object is the heaviest?** _____

4. **Which object is the lightest?** _____

5. **Which object is the roundest?** _____

6. **Which object is the crispiest?** _____

7. **Which object is the sharpest?** _____

8. **Which object is the hardest?** _____

Bonus: Write three EST sentences using any of the objects found above.

GA1347

Matching Shapes

Refer to the six shapes found below to answer each question.

1.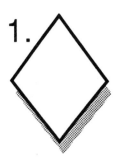

2.

3.

4.

5.

6.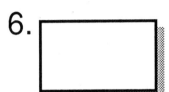

1. **Name a toy that is shaped like number one.** _____

2. **Name a food that is shaped almost like number three.** _____

3. **Name a food that is shaped like number two.** _____

4. **Name a sport that is played on a field shaped like number one.** _____

5. **Name a place you could find fifty shapes like number five.** _____

6. **Name a toy that is shaped like number two.** _____

7. **Name something you see in campgrounds that is shaped like number four.** _____

8. **Name a sport that is played on a field shaped like number six.** _____

9. **Name an animal that is shaped like number five.** _____

Bonus: Name something that is shaped like each of the six shapes pictured above.

GA1347

Make Your List

To make the treats pictured below, what would you need? Make a list of ingredients for each one.

1. peanut butter and jelly sandwich

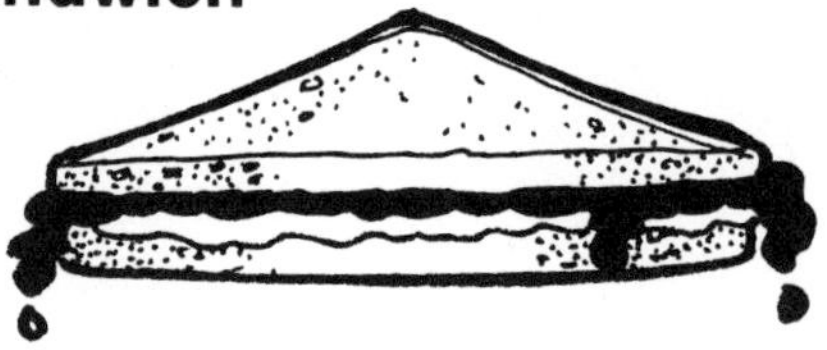

_____

_____

_____

2. popcorn balls

_____

_____

_____

3. banana split

_____

_____

_____

4. hamburger

_____

_____

_____

5. chocolate chip cookies

_____

_____

_____

6. hot chocolate

_____

_____

_____

Bonus: Write the step-by-step directions for making one of the treats pictured above.

Complete the Chart

Write the appropriate vegetable, fruit, animal, toy, or candy in each space on the chart. Example: A roundish vegetable is a pea, so the word *pea* has been placed in the first space. A candy that would fit in your pocket is a jaw breaker, so the words *jaw breaker* are found in the last space on the chart.

	Vegetable	Fruit	Animal	Toy	Candy
Roundish	PEA				
Heavier than most					
Green					
Long and thin					
Red					
Lighter than an apple					
Begins with the letter _L_					
Would fit in your pocket					JAW BREAKER

Bonus: Think of yet another category and write it in the space after, "Would fit in your pocket." Then complete the last line of the chart.

31

GA1347

Pick Only One!

Use one of the three words *all*, *some* or *none* to complete each sentence found below. Sometimes there will be more than one correct answer. Think and choose the answer that is the most correct.

1. _____ animals have four legs.

2. _____ trees have leaves.

3. _____ apples are green.

4. _____ shoes have shoelaces.

5. _____ ice cubes are frozen.

6. _____ people like to laugh.

7. _____ giraffes have long necks.

8. _____ children can swim.

Bonus: Write a true ALL, SOME, and MOST sentence.

GA1347

Pick a Tie, Any Tie

Begin this page by using crayons to decorate each of the four ties found below. Decorate each differently, using different colors and designs. Using the number for each tie, answer the questions found below.

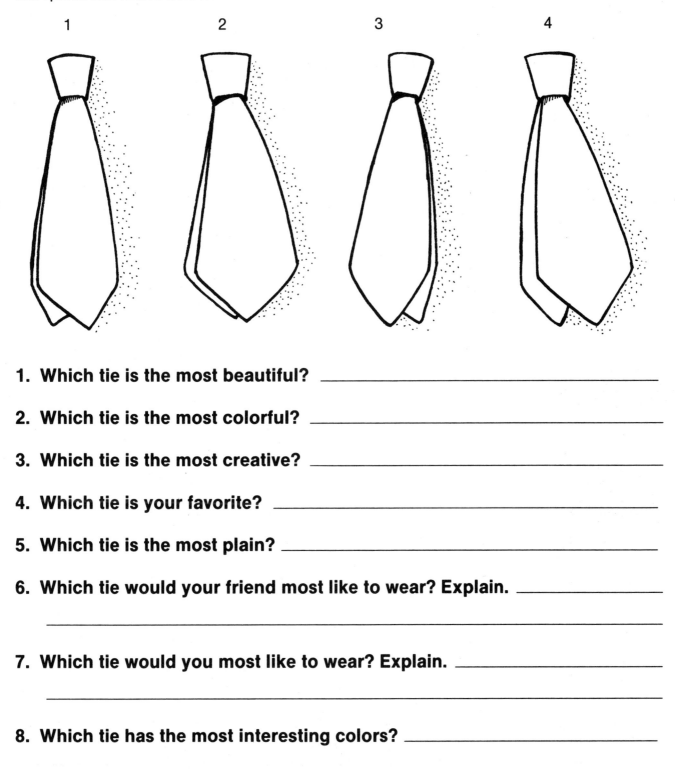

1. **Which tie is the most beautiful?** _____

2. **Which tie is the most colorful?** _____

3. **Which tie is the most creative?** _____

4. **Which tie is your favorite?** _____

5. **Which tie is the most plain?** _____

6. **Which tie would your friend most like to wear? Explain.** _____

    _____

7. **Which tie would you most like to wear? Explain.** _____

    _____

8. **Which tie has the most interesting colors?** _____

Bonus: List five uses for a tie, besides wearing it around your neck under a shirt collar.

Animal Facts

Use the six words *all*, *some*, *none*, *always*, *sometimes* and *never* to write sentences about the four animals pictured below.

1. **ALL** _____

_____

2. **SOME** _____

_____

3. **NONE** _____

_____

4. **ALWAYS** _____

_____

5. **SOMETIMES** _____

_____

6. **NEVER** _____

_____

Bonus: Use the words *often*, *rarely*, and *occasionally* to write three more facts about the four animals pictured above.

Check, Please

Use a check mark to indicate the appropriate classifications for each object listed on the chart. Example: A cork will float, so put a check mark in the very first space. A banana is edible, so put a check in the very last space on the chart.

	floats	attracted by magnet	will fit in pocket	edible
cork				
feather				
marshmallow				
refrigerator door				
wood chips				
fork				
pencil				
paper clip				
clock				
banana				

Bonus: Add one more object to the bottom of the chart and put appropriate check marks where needed.

Four Kids

Look at the picture carefully as you answer the questions below.

1. **Which child will probably get tired first?** _____

2. **Which child do you think needs a partner?** _____

3. **Which child would be able to carry his/her game in his/her pocket?**

   _____

4. **Which child is about to make 2 points?** _____

Bonus: Name a game which needs three people to play.

GA1347

How They Relate

Begin this page by carefully reading the incomplete sentences found below. Think about how the first two things relate to each other, then complete each sentence found below.

1. **A SHOE is to a FOOT as a GLOVE is to a** _____ .

2. **A HAND is to an ARM as a FOOT is to a** _____ .

3. **FOUR is to a CAT as TWO is to a** _____ .

4. **INK is to PEN as PAINT is to a** _____ .

5. **A HORN is to a BULL as an ANTLER is to a** _____ .

6. **SKIN is to MAN as FEATHERS are to a** _____ .

7. **ROUND is to an APPLE as SQUARE is to a** _____ .

8. **HOT is to STOVE as COLD is to a** _____ .

Bonus: Write one sentence that compares two sets of things that relate to each other in the same way.

Happy Birthday, John

John received three presents for his birthday. One was a watch, one was a bubble gum machine and the other was a frog. Use the facts found below to draw the appropriate present on each of the three boxes.

FACTS:

1. **The present is the first box is alive.**
2. **The present in the last box doesn't tell time.**

Bonus: If the facts were changed to read:

1. The present in the first box isn't alive.
2. The frog is in the first or last box.

What box contains the frog?

GA1347

Three Rabbits

Ralph has three rabbits. One is black, one is brown and one is white. Use the facts and complete the chart found below to decide what color each rabbit should be colored.

FACTS:
1. **The brown rabbit is in the first or last box.**
2. **The white rabbit isn't in either of the first two boxes.**

	brown	black	white
box 1			
box 2			
box 3			

Bonus: If the first fact was changed to read:

1. The brown rabbit isn't in the first or last box.

What box is the black rabbit in?

GA1347

Three Hats

Three children named Beth, Marty and Chris are each wearing hats. The hats are red, green and yellow. Use the facts and complete the chart found below to color each hat the correct color.

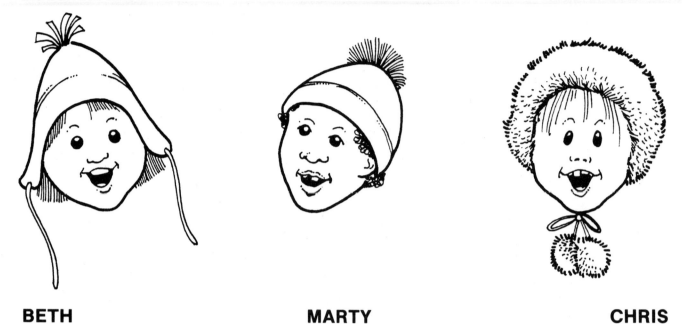

BETH   **MARTY**   **CHRIS**

FACTS:
1. Beth is wearing a yellow or green hat.
2. Chris is wearing a yellow hat if Marty is wearing a red hat. Or Chris is wearing a green hat if Beth is wearing a red hat.

	red	green	yellow
Beth			
Marty			
Chris			

Bonus: If the first fact is changed to read:
1. Beth is not wearing a yellow or a green hat.
What color hat would Marty then be wearing?

GA1347

Pick a Pet

Three children named Ruth, Judy and Mark have pets. The pets are a cat, a bird and a rat. Use the facts and complete the chart found below to draw a line connecting each child with his or her pet.

RUTH

JUDY

MARK

FACTS:
1. **Judy doesn't keep her pet in a cage.**
2. **Mark has the cat or the rat.**

	bird	cat	rat
Ruth			
Judy			
Mark			

Bonus: If the second fact was changed to read:
2. Mark doesn't own the cat or rat. Who owns the rat?

GA1347

The Picnic

Three children named Ray, Robin and Ricky went on a picnic. Each child brought one of the foods for the picnic. The children brought sandwiches, cupcakes and watermelon. Use the facts and complete the chart found below to draw what each child brought to the picnic.

FACTS:

1. **Ray brought watermelon or cupcakes.**
2. **Robin brought sandwiches or cupcakes.**
3. **If Ray brought the watermelon, Robin brought the cupcakes. If Ray brought the sandwiches, Ricky brought the cupcakes.**

Ray			
Robin			
Ricky			

Bonus: Choose the names of two friends and three picnic foods and write a puzzle like the one above. Provide facts and a chart. See if one of your two friends can solve your puzzle.

GA1347

Jones' Elementary School

Three people named Mrs. Brown, Mrs. White and Mr. Blue work at Jones' Elementary School. One is the kindergarten teacher, one is the janitor and one is the principal. Use the facts and complete the chart below to color each door the color of the correct person's name.

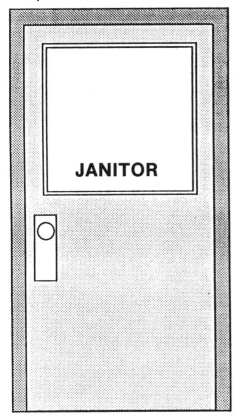

FACTS:
1. Mrs. Brown is a teacher or a janitor.
2. Mr. Blue is a teacher or a principal.
3. The principal is a lady.

	teacher	janitor	principal
Brown			
White			
Blue			

Bonus: If fact three was changed to read:

3. The principal is a man.

Who taught kindergarten?

What's for Lunch?

Three boys named Charles, Jason and Jered ate lunch together. One boy ate a hot dog, one ate pizza and one ate a hamburger. Use the facts and complete the chart found below to name each boy pictured below.

CHARLES   **JASON**   **JERED**

FACTS:
1. Charles ate a hot dog or pizza.
2. Jason ate pizza or a hamburger.
3. Jered ate a hot dog or pizza.
4. Charles' lunch had cheese.

Charles			
Jason			
Jered			

Bonus: If the fourth fact was changed to read:
4. Charles' lunch was not round.
Who ate the pizza for lunch?

GA1347

Favorite Colors

Three children named Jennifer, Jerry and Polly are discussing their favorite colors: red, blue or yellow. Use the facts and complete the chart found below to color each child's shirt his or her favorite color.

POLLY   **JERRY**   **JENNIFER**

FACTS:
1. Jerry said, "My favorite color is either red or blue."
2. Jennifer said, "My favorite color is red."
3. None of the children have the same favorite color.

	red	yellow	blue
Polly			
Jerry			
Jennifer			

Bonus: If fact three was changed to read:

3. All of the children have the same favorite color.

What color is Jerry's favorite?

GA1347

Colorful Locks

Three children named Olga, Egbert and Sue are brothers and sisters. Two of the children are twins. Each child has either long, curly red hair or short, straight brown hair. Use the facts and complete the chart found below to decide how to draw and color each child's hair.

| EGBERT | OLGA | SUE |

FACTS:
1. **Olga doesn't have brown hair like her twin.**
2. **Sue's hair isn't the same color as her big sister's.**

	long, curly, red	short, straight, brown
Olga		
Egbert		
Sue		

Bonus: Write a puzzle about three children and the color of their eyes.

GA1347

Caps and Socks

There are two brothers named Wally and Robert. One brother is wearing a red cap and the other is wearing a blue cap. One is wearing green socks and one is wearing orange socks. Use the facts and complete the chart found below to color each boys' cap and socks the correct colors?

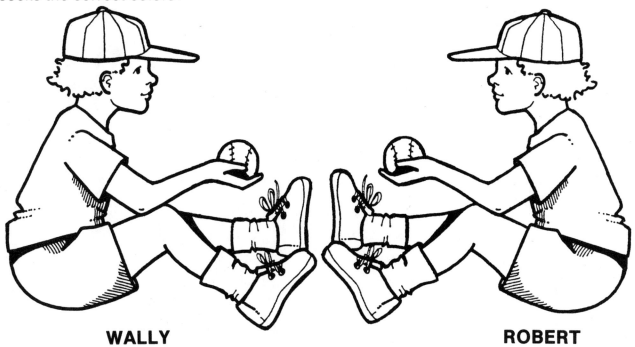

WALLY   **ROBERT**

FACTS:
1. **Wally is wearing a red cap and orange socks or he is wearing a blue cap and green socks.**
2. **Robert is not wearing green socks.**

	caps		socks	
	red	**blue**	**green**	**orange**
Wally				
Robert				

Bonus: If the second fact was changed to read:

2. Robert is not wearing a blue cap.

What color socks is Wally wearing?

How Did Misty Know?

There are three girls named Misty, Lisa and Kim. There are five hats. Three are black and two are white. The girls can see the hats worn by the other two girls but each girl cannot see her own hat or the two unworn hats. Use the fact found below to color each girl's hat the correct color.

MISTY   **LISA**   **KIM**

FACT:

Misty looked at the other two girls' hats and said, "I know the color of my hat and the color of the two hats that no one is wearing."

Bonus: Explain how Misty knew the color of her hat.

GA1347

Changing Hats

There are three children named Ron, Sharon and Jim. There are five hats, two red and three blue. Each child can see the hats worn by his/her two friends but cannot see his/her own hat or the two unworn hats. Use the facts found below to determine what color hat Ron is wearing.

RON **SHARON** **JIM**

FACTS:
1. **Looking at the hats worn by Ron and Jim, Sharon said, "I cannot determine the color of my hat."**
2. **Looking at the hats worn by Sharon and Ron, Jim said, "I cannot determine the color of my hat either."**
3. **Ron said, "Although I do not see both red hats, I can still determine the color of my hat, because of what Jim said.**

Bonus: Explain how Ron knew the color of his hat.

Double Trouble

Three children, Eric, Amy and Sarah, each received a new toy. One child received a wagon, one received a bike and the other received a tricycle. Each of the toys was either red or blue. Use the facts found below to color and tag each of the toys found below.

FACTS:

1. Eric's new toy didn't have four wheels, but it was blue.
2. Amy's toy had two wheels.
3. Sarah's toy wasn't the same color as Eric and Amy's toy.

	wagon		bike		tricycle	
	blue	**red**	**blue**	**red**	**blue**	**red**
Eric						
Amy						
Sarah						

Bonus: Which fact tells the color of Eric's toy?

Flowers for Teacher

Three girls named Rose, Lily and Daisy brought flowers to their teacher. One girl brought roses, one brought lilies and one brought daisies. Use the facts and complete the chart found below to complete the gift tags.

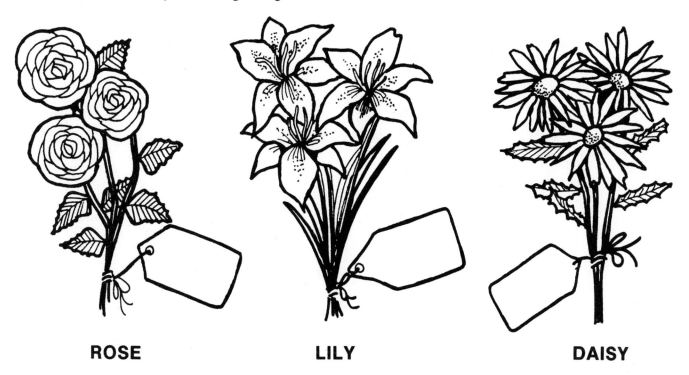

ROSE   LILY   DAISY

FACTS:
  1. **None of the girls brought a flower that was the same as her name.**
  2. **Daisy brought the lilies or daisies.**

	roses	lilies	daisies
Rose			
Lily			
Daisy			

Bonus: If the second fact was changed to read:

2. Daisy or Rose brought the roses.

Who would have brought the lilies?

Bake Sale

Three girls, Barbara, Julie, and Alison, baked foods for the Girl Scout bake sale. One girl baked cupcakes, one baked brownies and one baked a lemon cake. Use the facts and complete the chart found below to label each food pictured below.

BAKED BY:

CUPCAKES COMPLIMENTS OF:

BROWNIES BY:

FACTS:
1. Alison brought the brownies or the lemon cake.
2. Barbara brought the brownies or the lemon cake.
3. If Julie brought the cupcakes, then Barbara brought the lemon cake. But if Julie didn't bring the cupcakes, then Alison brought the lemon cake.

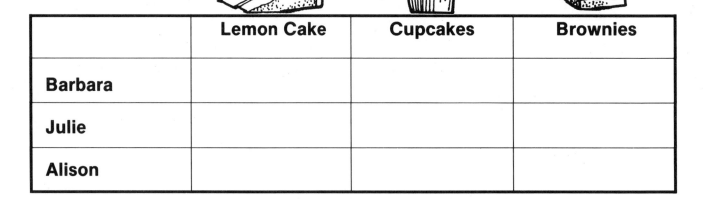

	Lemon Cake	Cupcakes	Brownies
Barbara			
Julie			
Alison			

Bonus: Write a puzzle like this one using the names of your three favorite bake sale items and the names of your three best friends.

GA1347

Spotted Rabbits

Cheryl has three spotted rabbits. One rabbit is white, one is black and one is brown. One rabbit has black spots, one rabbit has brown spots and one rabbit has white spots. Use the facts and the chart found below to color the rabbits the correct colors.

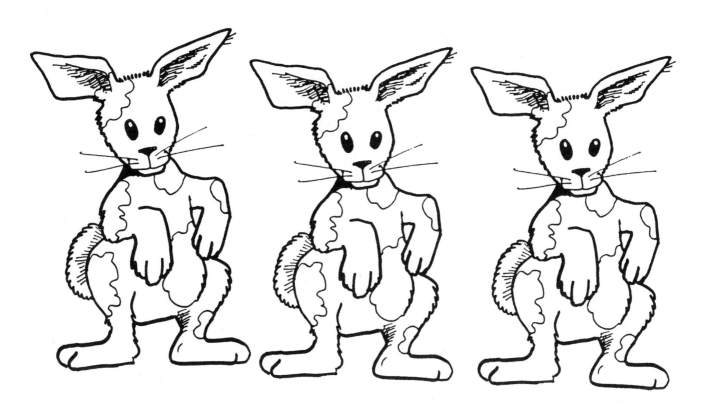

FACTS:
1. **The white rabbit doesn't have brown spots.**
2. **The brown rabbit doesn't have black spots.**

	black spots	brown spots	white spots
white			
black			
brown			

Bonus: If the first fact read:
1. The white rabbit doesn't have black spots.

What color spots would the brown rabbit have?

Gary's Shirts

Gary has three striped shirts. One shirt is blue, one is red and one is yellow. The stripes on the shirts are either purple, green or orange. Use the facts and complete the chart found below to decide what color to color each of the three shirts found below.

FACTS:
1. **The yellow shirt has orange stripes.**
2. **The blue shirt has orange or green stripes.**
3. **The red shirt has purple or orange stripes.**

	purple	green	orange
blue			
red			
yellow			

Bonus: If the second fact was changed to read:
2. The blue shirt has orange or purple stripes.

What color stripes would the red shirt have?

GA1347

Lunch Out

Three boys named Bernard, Zac and Peter went out for lunch. One boy drank milk, one drank soda and one drank a shake. One boy ate a burger, one ate pizza and one ate a hot dog. Use the facts and complete the chart found below to determine what each boy ate and drank.

FACTS:
1. **The boy who ate the burger drank a soda.**
2. **The boy who ate pizza didn't drink a shake.**
3. **Bernard drank milk.**
4. **Peter didn't eat a burger.**

	milk	soda	shake	burger	pizza	hot dog
Bernard						
Zac						
Peter						

Bonus: If facts three and four were changed to read:

3. Bernard drank a soda.
4. Peter didn't eat pizza.
What did Zac eat and drink?

GA1347

Answer Key

Sorting It Out! page 5
Answers may vary.
1. carrot/pumpkin
2. balloon/ball
3. apple/orange
4. lemon/pickle (both sour)
5. pencil/pen
6. file/sand paper (rough)

You Decide page 6
1. A, D
2. B, C
3. A, D, E
4. A, B, C, D
5. A, E
6. A, B, C, D, E, F
Bonus: Both begin with the letter *C*.

Putting It in Order page 7
   2, 4, 1, 3, 6, 5
Bonus: (May vary.)
7. Sprinkle with sugar and cinnamon.
8. Chill in refrigerator.

Similarities page 8
1. color
2. weight
3. shape
4. size

What's Next? page 9
1. heart
2. X
3. triangle
4. heart
5. starburst
6. triangle
7. circle
8. X
Bonus: The star.

Pick Carefully page 10
Answers may vary, discuss each one.
1. 1, 3, 6
2. 1, 3, 4, 5, 6
3. 2, 3, 4
4. 5, 6
5. 1, 2, 4, 5
6. 2
Bonus: They are food, small, and eaten at ball games.
They are different colors, textures and tastes.

Calendar Work page 11
1. Monday
2. Tuesday
3. Sunday
4. Tuesday
5. Wednesday
6. Tuesday
Bonus: Tuesday

Putting It Together page 12
1. pizza
2. jack-o'-lantern
3. chocolate chip cookies
4. Cracker Jacks

Always, Sometimes, Never page 13
1. 3   5. 2
2. 6   6. 3
3. 5   7. 1
4. 4   8. 5 or 6

Or, And, Not page 14
1. and   5. or
2. not   6. not
3. and   7. not
4. or   8. and

Picture It! page 15
Bonus: B3

Color It First! page 16
1. 2,5
2. 1,4
3. 3,5
4. 6
5. 2
6. 3,6
7. 2,3
Bonus:

Add One page 17
1. little red triangle
2. big blue circle
3. smaller red circle
4. big blue triangle
5. smaller red triangle
6. small red square

All, Most, Some, None page 18
1. all
2. most
3. some
4. none
5. some
6. all
7. none
8. some

Chosen Colors page 19
1. most
2. some, most
3. none
4. some
5. all
6. some
7. none
8. all
Bonus: red

Size, Shape and Weight page 20
Answers may vary, discuss possibilities.
1. 3
2. 1
3. 3
4. 5
5. 2
6. 5
7. 3
8. 3, 1, 4, 2, 6, 5
Bonus: 2, 3, 4, 1, 6, 5

Button, Button page 21
1. 6
2. 3
3. 4
4. 2
5. 1
6. 5

Six Kids page 22
1. all
2. all
3. all
4. none
5. all
6. none

Just Three, Please page 23
1. popcorn, pan, heat
2. caramels, apples, heat
3. sugar, flour, chocolate chips
4. two sticks, paper, string

GA1347

Draw Them! page 25
Answers may vary. These are just suggestions:
1. glue
2. cotton candy
3. boiling water
4. pickle
5. chili
6. ice cubes
Bonus: hot fudge sundae

Just Before page 26
Answers may vary.
1. put on socks
2. unwrap it/open mouth
3. put on skates
4. put on gloves
5. take off clothes/step in tub
6. put paste on brush/open mouth
7. close eyes
8. open the book

The First Thing page 27
1. I stretch in bed.
2. I put on my shoes.
3. I dry my hands.
4. I take my hand off my heart.
5. I walk in the door.
6. I sit down to watch.
7. I open my desk.
8. I begin to read.

Est, Est, Est! page 28
1. 1
2. 3
3. 1
4. 3
5. 5
6. 6
7. 4
8. 2

Matching Shapes page 29
Answers may vary.
1. kite
2. slice of bread
3. pie
4. baseball
5. American flag
6. ball
7. tents
8. tennis
9. starfish

Make Your List page 30
Answers may vary.
1. peanut butter, bread, jelly
2. popcorn, caramel
3. banana, ice cream, toppings
4. bun, hamburger patty, pickle, ketchup
5. chcoclate chips, flour, sugar, butter, eggs
6. milk, cocoa mix

Complete the Chart page 31
Answers may vary.

Pick Only One! page 32
1. some
2. some
3. some
4. some
5. all
6. some
7. all
8. some

Pick a Tie, Any Tie page 33
Answers may vary.

Animal Facts page 34
1. All of the animals above live on this earth.
2. Some of the animals have four legs.
3. None of the animals can fly.
4. The animals always need to eat.
5. The animals like to sleep sometimes.
6. The animals above never drive cars.

Check, Please page 35

cork	✓		✓	
feather	✓		✓	
marshmallow	✓		✓	✓
refrigerator door		✓		
wood chips	✓		✓	
fork		✓	✓	
pencil	✓			
paper clip			✓	✓
clock			✓	
banana			✓	✓

Four Kids page 36
1. 1
2. 3
3. 4
4. 2
Bonus: Answers may vary.

How They Relate page 37
1. hand
2. leg
3. bird, human
4. brush
5. elk, deer, moose, etc.
6. bird
7. box
8. freezer

Happy Birthday, John page 38
box 1. frog
box 2. watch
box 3. gumball machine
Deductions: Fact 1 tells us that the frog is in the first box. Fact 2 tells us that the last box isn't the watch, so the watch must be in the second box. The bubble gum must be in the last box.
Bonus: box 3

Three Rabbits page 39
box 1. brown
box 2. black
box 3. white
Deductions: Fact 1 tells us that the brown rabbit is not in the second box. Fact 2 tells us that the white rabbit is in the last box. If the white rabbit is in the third box and the second box isn't the brown rabbit, the black rabbit must be in the second box. That leaves the first box for the brown rabbit.
Bonus: first box

Three Hats page 40
Beth: green
Marty: red
Chris: yellow
Deductions: Fact 1 tells us that Beth is not wearing the red hat. Fact 2 tells us that Chris is wearing yellow and Marty is wearing red, OR Chris is wearing green and Beth is wearing red. We know that Beth is not wearing red, so the first part is true—Chris is wearing yellow an Marty is wearing red. Therefore, both must be wearing green.
Bonus: yellow

Pick a Pet page 41
Ruth: bird
Judy: cat
Mark: rat
Deductions: Fact 1 tells us that Judy has the cat. (Birds and rats are kept in cages.) Fact 2 tells us that Mark has the cat or rat, but we already know that Judy has the cat, so Mark must have the rat. Therefore, Ruth has the bird.
Bonus: Ruth

The Picnic page 42
Ray: watermelon
Robin: cupcakes
Ricky: sandwiches
Deductions: Fact 1 tells us that Ray did not bring the sandwiches. Fact 2 tells us that Robin did not bring the watermelon. Fact 3 tells us that Ray brought watermelon and Robin brought cupcakes, OR Ray brought sandwiches and Ricky brought cupcakes. We know that from Fact 1 that Ray didn't bring the sandwiches; therefore, Ray brought watermelon and Robin brought cupcakes. That leaves sandwiches for Ricky.

GA1347

Jones' Elementary School page 43
White: principal
Blue: teacher
Brown: janitor
Deductions: Fact 1 tells us that Brown is not the principal. Fact 2 tells us that Blue is not the janitor. Fact 3 tells us that the principal is a woman, and Fact 2 said Mrs. Brown wasn't a principal, therefore, Mrs. White must be the principal. Fact 2 said Mr. Blue wasn't the janitor and he cannot be the principal, therefore, Mr. Blue must be the teacher. That leaves Mrs. Brown to be the janitor.
Bonus: Mrs. White

What's for Lunch? page 44
Charles: pizza
Jason: hamburger
Jered: hot dog
Deductions: Fact 1 tells us that Charles did not eat the hamburger. Fact 2 tells us that Jason did not eat the hot dog. Fact 3 tells us that Jered did not eat the hamburger. Fact 4 tells us that Charles ate the pizza and Fact 1 determined that he didn't have a hamburger. If Charles ate the pizza, Jason must have had the hamburger. (See fact 2.) Therefore, Jered must have eaten the hot dog.
Bonus: Jered

Favorite Colors page 45
Polly: yellow
Jerry: blue
Jennifer: red
Deductions: Fact 1 tells us that Jerry's favorite color is not yellow. Fact 2 tells us that Jennifer's favorite color is red. Fact 3 tells us that each child has a different favorite color, therefore Jerry's favorite color must be blue. (See fact 1.) Therefore that leaves yellow as the favorite color for Polly.
Bonus: red

Colorful Locks page 46
Egbert and Olga are twins. Sue is the little sister. Egbert and Sue have short, straight, brown hair. Olga has long, curly, red hair.
Deductions: Fact 1 tells us that Olga is a twin and that she has long, curly, red hair. Fact 2 tells us that Sue is the little sister and she has short, straight, brown hair. From Fact 1 we can now determine that Olga's twin is Egbert and he has short, straight, brown hair like Sue.

Caps and Socks page 47
Wally: blue cap/green socks
Robert: red cap/orange socks
Deductions: Fact 1 tells us that one of the boys is wearing red cap and orange socks or blue cap and green socks. Fact 2 tells us that Robert is not wearing green socks; therefore, he is wearing the orange socks and red cap. That leaves Wally wearing the blue cap and green socks.
Bonus: Doesn't change the color of the boys caps or socks.

How Did Misty Know? page 48
Misty: black
Lisa: white
Kim: white
Deductions: Misty must have seen both of the white hats and knew she was wearing one of the other three black hats.
Bonus: See deductions above.

Changing Hats page 49
Ron: blue
Sharon: red
Jim: blue
Deductions: Fact 1 tells us that Sharon does not see both of the red hats. Fact 2 tells us that Jim doesn't see red hats. Fact 3 tell us that Ron doesn't see two red hats, but since he knows the color of his hat from what Jim said, he must see Sharon wearing a red hat and Jim wearing a blue hat. Since he knows the color of his hat by what Jim says, he must know that Jim sees one red hat (worn by Sharon) and he doesn't see a second red hat worn by Ron. Therefore, Ron knew that he was not wearing a red hat and must be wearing a blue hat.
Bonus: See deductions above.

Double Trouble page 50
Eric: blue/tricycle
Amy: blue/bike
Sarah: red/wagon
Deductions: Fact 1 tells us Eric has a blue tricycle or a blue bike. Fact 2 tells us that Amy has the bike; therefore, Eric must have a blue tricycle, which leaves the wagon for Sarah. Fact 3 tells us that Sarah's toy isn't blue like Eric's, so the wagon must be red. It also tells us Amy's toy is the same color as Eric's, therefore, Amy's bike is blue.

Flowers for Teacher page 51
Rose: daisies
Lily: roses
Daisy: lilies
Deductions: Fact 1 tells us that Rose brought daisies or roses, Lily brought daisies or roses and Daisy brought roses or lilies. Fact 2 tells us that Daisy brought lilies or daisies and Fact 1 has already determined that she didn't bring the daisies, therefore, Daisy brought the lilies. Rose couldn't have brought the roses; therefore she brought the daisies. Lily is left with the roses.
Bonus: Rose

Bake Sale page 52
Barbara: lemon cake
Julie: cupcakes
Alison: brownies
Deductions: Fact 1 tells us that Alison did not bring the cupcakes. Fact 2 tells us that Barbara did not bring the cupcakes; therefore, Julie must have brought the cupcakes. Fact 3 tells us that if Julie brought cupcakes (proven already) then Barbara brought the lemon cake. That leaves Alison and the brownies.

Spotted Rabbits page 53
white rabbit with black spots
black rabbit with brown spots
brown rabbit with white spots
Deductions: If the white rabbit doesn't have brown spots, it must have black spots. The brown rabbit doesn't has black spots, so it must have white spots. That leaves brown spots for the black rabbit.
Bonus: white

Gary's Shirts page 54
blue with green stripes
red with purple stripes
yellow with orange stripes
Deductions: Fact 1 tells us that the yellow shirt has orange stripes. Fact 2 tells us that the blue shirt doesn't have purple stripes. Fact 3 tells us that the red shirt has purple or orange stripes. Since fact 2 tells us that the blue shirt doesn't have purple stripes and we know that the orange stripes are on the yellow shirt, the blue shirt must have green stripes. That leaves the red shirt and purple stripes.
Bonus: green

Lunch Out page 55
Bernard: pizza/milk
Zac: burger/soda
Peter: hot dog/shake
Deductions: Fact 1 tells us that the burger and soda go together. Fact 2 tells us that pizza and milk go together. That leaves the hot dog and shake. Now we know how the foods are paired together. The next step is to determine which boy had each combination. Fact 3 tells us that Bernard drank milk, therefore, he ate pizza. Fact 4 tells us that Peter must have had the hot dog; therefore, he drank a shake. That leaves Zac and the burger and soda.
Bonus: pizza and milk

GA1347

59

GA1347

Certificate of Award
GOOD THINKING!!

For _____

_____   _____
Date   **Signature**

BONUS
Award
Certificate

To _____

_____

To _____

_____